Behind Heaven's Curtains

By Jaclyn R. Majer

PublishAmerica
Baltimore

First printing

Photography for book cover by Ron Simon, Calgary, Alberta, Canada

ISBN: 1-4137-8422-4
PUBLISHED BY PUBLISHAMERICA, LLLP
www.publishamerica.com
Baltimore

Printed in the United States of America

Dedication

I would like to dedicate this book to my mother, Norma Keegan, who taught me about these heavenly beings as a child with my first prayer to my guardian angel. And to my father, Jimmy Keegan, who went to his eternal rest when I was only thirteen, but never really left, because he is still so close, guiding and protecting me here. Now both in heaven, you are my special angels. I love you and I thank you. This book is for you, so you will know I hear you, and I know I am not alone.

Acknowledgments

I would like to acknowledge my family—my husband Jim, daughters Jaime and Lisa and her husband Demetri, and our granddaughter Alexia, my stepson Mathew and his wife Tammy, and our grandchildren Daelyn and Haley, for their love and inspiration. Angels do walk on this planet, right here, right now. I'm so grateful to have all of you in my life.

Table of Contents

Introduction

Sometimes it's good to rest a while and look inward, listen to that inner world where real truth lives. And when we do, if we're lucky and the time is right, we may just glimpse, or hear, a tiny voice bringing us messages of love to lift us up and make us feel better; to bring life and happiness into an otherwise troubled world.

Behind Heaven's Curtains is truly an angelic experience winged to you by the angels themselves, out of love and concern, in this drastically changing world. Angels are all around us and sometimes, when the moment is right, we can hear and even see their heavenly forms. They are here when times are happy and also when they're sad, because angels are not fair-weather friends. They have chosen to be our guides, and accompany us on the whole long journey through this life. Sometimes we can feel them near us and sometimes we just know, but the important thing to realize is just that—they're here, all around us, a very real part of this world.

Here are messages sent by them to you, so you will know with all certainty they see, they know what is happening in our lives, and they care. Angels aren't just paintings on gothic cathedral walls and stained glass windows; they are real, vibrant, and alive. They are speaking to us now to let us know we are not alone.

Behind Heaven's Curtains addresses the everyday life in the here and now, so don't be surprised should you find they have changed somewhat from the old, traditional concepts of angels.

Hush now and listen to that tiny voice of love surrounding you, caressing you, and trying with all their hearts to help you feel and know that everything will be alright. Reach inward. Maybe you will even hear them whisper, "You're not alone."

Behind Heaven's Curtains

Softly, gently ,flows the sea,
And softly, gently, brings the breeze
That shifts so lightly with the sands
Of time and love, of far off lands.

We wonder what awaits us there
Beyond the curtains sheer and fair,
Where angels live and saints abide,
And all but Heavenly Father hides.

We try again, yet we can't see
All the wonders through the scree
Of golden, filmy, billowing mist
That hides the secrets from our grasp.

And softly, gently, you and I,
We wait and watch and then we sigh,
Is there yet no way to see
Behind the veil of centuries?

Is there yet no way to know
Where angels live, where heaven grows
All the blessing stored in circles,
Hidden in His cup of miracles?

So softly, gently, we do glimpse
Across the eons, through the mist
To where all prayers and secrets live,
To where the Heavenly Father gives...

Life and love unto us all,
And beauty bright when ashes fall
From bodies here, to wings beyond,
We cross through paradise's fronds.

Then softly, gently, yet we'll see
The sacred home of angels be
Too close to see, too far to pass,
Yet it lies here within our grasp.

The mist, it drifts and sways and swirls,
And gossamer threads they do unfurl.
Through a crack in time we chance to see
Beyond the veil, the curtain, free.

Softly, softly, yet it flows
Across my cheek, and then it blows
Away like thistle made of down,
To lift and sway and not be found.

Gather 'Round

Hushing whispers on the wind.
Joy and love around their wings.
Angels bend to touch his head,
And gently rock his little bed.

"Oh look, how new he really is."
Bends and gives a little kiss.
Another lifts the cover thin,
To tuck beneath his little chin.

Another rings a little bell
To tell the world that all is well.
He has arrived here safe and sound.
They have prepared his little crown.

Together they bow and say a prayer,
"Father above, protect him here.
He's very new in this dark place.
Please, fill his life with love and grace.

"We'll be around him all day long,
And in the night we'll keep him strong.
And from his path if he should roam,
We'll stay close by to bring him home."

They bow their heads and close their eyes.
The air is filled with lullabies.
And baby grins to…no one there,
Just angels floating in the air.

The Little Ones

I hear the sounds of violins and strains of mystic songs.
I see the light of candles glow behind the forest fronds.
And deep within the jungle vines where lions and tigers roam
I feel a deep regretful awe that they feel all alone.

A song is singing in my heart; a song without an end.
I watch and wait while others ponder what to do with him.
My heart it beats within my breast and sorrow fills the air.
Where are the champions of my kin, the lions proud and fair?

Where are the kings of those who swim beneath the waters deep,
Where dolphins swirl and coo and chirp with promises to keep.
And when the sun begins to fall behind the people's mall,
Where are the ones with love so strong to answer their sad call?

The lion proud, the bear and deer, the elephant so grand,
They are a lovely, secret part of Father's wondrous plan,
But what becomes of lives so true where animals abide,
When trophies are the just rewards for hunters where they hide?

And what will come of all the dreams where they play such a part
To calm the souls of all mankind and justly do their part,
To fill the world with wonder, and to soak our hearts with grace.
Do they deserve a home that's safe, a warm and quiet place?

Search then within your heart of hearts and ponder of the cause,
When man is the true animal and justice lags in pause.
So send the angels' "light" and "love" unto these creatures 'til,
They find their freedom and their peace, and all their hearts are still.

Angel's Wings

Hush. Listen to the whisper,
Feel the brush against your cheek.
Feel the tiny gasp of lightness
That fills you with relief.

That's your angel's wing caressing
To lightly touch your very soul.
It's a little hope and prayer,
A drop of love to fill the hole.

Bow Your Head

When you shove away the outside
And reach deep within your soul,
When you lift your mind to grandness,
To the Father tell your goals.

When you wish for peace in living
And some joy to fill the void,
Ask your angel for assistance.
Quell the rabble and the noise.

Bow your heads in prayer together.
Send your message on his wings.
He understand your hopes and fears,
Has a feeling for these things.

He'll whisper to the Father
In heaven up above,
And bring you back the priceless gift
Of His eternal love.

Kindness

The water's still at evening time.
The loon calls out across the pines,
And deep within the forest still
A little bird begins to trill.

It seems she is disturbed tonight.
An egg has fallen and it might
Be stepped on by the men around,
And so she sings her sad, sad song.

The twigs begin to crack and click
Down low beneath her little nest.
And as she looks she sees him there,
Her egg held tenderly in his care.

He looks above. She looks down low.
Their eyes meet now and then she knows,
His kindness shines out from his heart,
And up the branches he does start.

Quickly she flits on up the tree
And watches, waits 'til it is free
For her to fly back down again,
And tend her egg, and watch it mend.

We are the little eggs you see;
The ones that fall from the tall pine tree.
The ones that wait precariously
For some kind soul to set us free.

Be kind to those who love you now,
But kinder yet to those who call
Out angrily to all who'll hear,
And fill the air with their dark fears.

Be kind to those of humble hearts,
And those who try to do their part,
Yet fail it seems at every turn.
Remember, in them His love burns.

Remember when you talk unkind
That someone's soul is bound and tied,
And someone's heart is hurt beyond
The bandages that your words have bound.

Be kind and unto you will come
Blessings endless like the sun,
Joys beyond the realm of reason.
Peace for every man and season.

Can You Hear Me?

Can you hear me when I whisper?
I try to every day,
But I see you walk before me
Full of problems and dismay.

I call you very often.
I try to lift you up,
But you just turn your back and cry,
You feel your life's too tough.

If only I could reach you.
I try to every day,
But you just turn your back again,
And slowly…walk away.

I knock, but you won't answer.
I call, but you don't hear.
I touch your stooping shoulder,
I brush you tousled hair.

I weep when you are weeping,
And I moan when you are down.
I want to help you learn to smile,
But you only seem to frown.

How can I bridge this distance,
How can I make you see,
That you are never all alone,
You have a friend…It's me.

I Will Lift You Up

When life's too much to handle,
When nothing goes just right,
When rain and wind and shadow
Block the path and feed the fight,

If only you will listen
I will drive away your pain.
I will lift you up to heaven,
I will be your dearest friend.

When everyone is angry
And hope is miles away,
When nothing in your life is right,
Don't give up and walk away.

I will lift you up to heaven.
I will fill your heart with love.
I will drive away the sadness
With His peace from up above.

Close your eyes for just a moment.
Close you eyes and you will see
That I am right beside you,
I don't want to let this be.

I will lift you up to heaven.
I will be your dearest friend.
I will clear the path to gladness,
Show you joy that has no end.

If only you will listen
I will drive away your pain.
I will lift you up, caress you.
I will be your dearest friend.

Tiny Stars

Let me take your tears of sadness,
Lift them high above the skies,
And place them in the heavens,
Tiny stars before your eyes.

Let me brush away forever
All the cares, and woes, and shame.
Look above you to the heavens.
The tiny stars, they call your name.

Crystal Children

There's a secret on the wind.
There's a miracle within.
And all around the children gather,
Waiting for the heavenly ladder
For the new ones coming now,
Who have the wisdom and the power,
To make the changes here on earth
And bring to us a royal birth.
Little ones so full of grace,
Little ones so fair of face,
You may begin your life anew,
This time with honour, tried and true.
You wake now from birth's long sleep,
Open your eyes and sneak a peek
At new and glorious waves of wonder,
Challenges are your goals and plunder.
You have come to save us all.
You are here to answer calls
Made long ago, in far off times.
You're here at last. All will be fine.

I Am an Angel

I am your guardian angel,
A messenger and friend.
I am the thought behind the act,
The caution in the end.

I am the wish for all that's good,
The evening prayer of peace.
I am the whisper on the wind,
The cuddle as you sleep.

I am the evening star above,
The waves upon the shore.
I am the vows for light and love,
The hope for peace and more.

I am a messenger, a guide,
A prayer from up above.
I am an angel made by Him,
But I am not…a God.

So lift your messages up to me,
I'll handle them with care.
I'll wing them up to heaven
To your God who's always there.

I am a messenger, a guide,
A prayer from up above.
I am an angel made by him,
But I am not…a God.

An Angel on Your Shoulder

There's an angel on your shoulder.
And then, someone would say,
"But look again, a devil
He lurks not far away."

"Look, there's a dove; a sign of peace.
Look then again, a war.
Is there an end to this unease,
This struggle at our core?"

There's an angel on your shoulder.
Well, I prefer to see him fair,
Rather than the devil
Who you say is lurking there.

There's war and struggle all around
But how can we survive,
If we focus on the evil ground
Where the sleeping dogs still lie?

For me, I'll stir the pot once more,
Route out the evil ways.
I'll push the darkness far from shore.
I'll fight for peaceful days.

Yes, there's an angel on my shoulder,
And I prefer to see him there.
Take the devil where you may my friend,
There is good…everywhere.

A Picture of Love

There's a golden glow around you,
A glow you cannot see.
It reaches out to touch you.
That form you see, is me.

For I pray not just with singing,
Nor with music, nor with words.
I pray with color and with light,
It's love that can't be heard.

The golden glow I wrap you in
Is light from up above.
A special gift I bring to you.
It's His eternal love.

The Search

Where are the answers, where do you seek?
How do you dig way down so deep?
We've always been told that God's all around
But you've looked, and you're sure that He just can't be found.

You've searched all the churches—they have all the words.
You're told how to feel, and you're told all the rules.
But where is the feeling, that love they speak of?
Is there really a path to the One up above?

It's easy to doubt and it's easy to blame,
Shut all the doors and dull all the pain.
There's doubt out there, pain, sorrow, and strife.
We feel that there's nothing unless there's a fight.

But it need not be so, we can rise above this,
Take charge of our lives. It's a prayer, not a wish.
Reach out to your angel, let him lift you above,
Bathe your world in hope, happiness, and love.

Have faith he is real. Have faith and he'll bring
Love and hope from the Father on his angel wings.
Let go of the doubt. Throw the anger away.
Take hold of his hand, and he'll lead the way.

Answers

We search the whole world over,
Turning every single stone.
There are very heavy problems here.
No answers to be found.

Everywhere there's toil and strife,
Turmoil at every turn.
Where's the hope we've heard about?
Where's the love that burns?

We ride the winds of anger.
We wield swords of despair.
We ask all those around us,
Is there anyone who cares?

And then a voice begins to raise
Up from our very souls,
A voice that says that there are ways
To find our long lost goals.

Your angel whispers quietly,
A secret deep within.
"The answers aren't out in the world.
The answers are with Him."

Seek instead the quiet,
The solitude and grace.
Look for peace and comfort.
Find a quiet place.

Bend your head and listen,
The answers are within.
The ones you seek are deep inside.
The answers are, with Him.

In Times to Come

The horse's hooves are thundering along the garden path.
Upon his back there rides a knight with lance and shield so fast.
And in the night as others sleep, he rides so hard and strong
To reach the long-lost mountain where the others wait ere' long.

The garden of the castle keep is quiet as he goes.
A muffled thunder stirred the air just once, and then it froze
Within the dreams of sleepers as they pass the hours away,
But he has many words to speak and messages this day.

And so he rides with all his heart up to the mountain high.
Behind the castle in the distance, others hear his cry,
"Make haste! Make haste! The armies ride not very far behind!"
And suddenly the night lights up with soldiers at his side.

"The time has come!" he calls to them from high upon his horse.
"We rest a bit and then we ride to conquer that great force
Where evil reigns and justice fails within the hands of law.
It is the time to end this madness. It is at last our call."

And knights of old they dawn their garb of crosses red and white,
And mount their steeds, their champions grand to ride into the night.
And angels sound their trumpets loud upon the mountain tall,
The time has come for all mankind to make his choice, or fall.

The time has come for you and me to ponder deep within,
Will we stand aside and watch as others sound the din?
Will we wait for others brave to stand up tall and grand?
Or will we stand ourselves right now, and follow God's great plan?

Hush Little One

Hush little baby as you drift
To dreamland in your little skift.
Your angel guides your boat along,
And keeps you safe and keeps you strong.

Hush little one. You close your eyes.
Your angel sings a lullaby,
A secret just for you and him.
You know. You answer with a grin.

An Angel's Choice

A war is here, an earthquake there,
A planet's face wracked with despair.
The people run as if possessed,
Trying to escape the recent pest.

If given a choice, would you be here
If you could be in heaven dear?
Our angels would. They really care.
They're with us, even in despair

Listen

Listen with your inner ear
For the sound that isn't there.
For the brush upon your hand,
And the hush upon the land.

Listen then to other things,
The wind, the water, the angel's wings.
How do you know they aren't there
If you've never listened deep in here?

Push your weary cares away
And listen in a deeper way,
For you'll never know the lovely part
If you don't listen with your heart.

Push Away

Like a boat upon the river,
Don't push away from the shore forever.
Instead, take a moment to decide
If you'd rather walk or ride.

If you'd rather swim or float?
Do you really need a boat?
Or is it just a little river
To sit beside and ponder whether…

Angels are here or over there,
Or are they really anywhere?
Push the boat out in the blue,
Then look above. He's guiding you.

Beauty of the Night

We look up to the starry night,
The moon so silver and so white.
The midnight blue is all around,
And peace and love can now be found.

What beauty is there more than this?
It could be an angel's kiss.
It could be her gentle wings
Or the music as she sings.

We look up to the starry night,
The moon so silver and so white.
The midnight blue is all around.
Our loving angels hold our crowns.

Take His Hand

When the road you're traveling is far too long,
When the trials you're fighting are far too strong,
When the cares are pressing you down so low
That you really don't know which way to go...

Stop for a second and retrace your steps.
You've forgotten a promise that will be kept.
He's been with you since you first began.
He's there…Reach up and take his hand.

His Wish

You are a breath of His very own,
But He never wished you to be all alone.
He called his messengers from on high
And each could hear a baby's sigh.

He sent his doves to circle there,
To watch your crib with loving care.
And to be sure that you were never alone,
An angel He sent, from His very home.

The Bells

Oh, can you hear the tinkling bells,
The tiny sounds like little shells,
The swishing noise of silk on lace,
Or the little grin on a baby's face?

The angel bends and blows a kiss,
A gentle breeze you could surely miss.
Crystals tinkle as the wind blows by.
His angel is singing a lullaby.

Tiny Pearls

Tiny pearls upon the sand.
Tiny petals in my hand.
Tiny tears on baby's face.
Tiny angels full of grace.

Let it Pass

When those around you make you frown,
When all the blue has turned to brown,
When the sun is hidden by darkened clouds,
And your need for solace is filled with crowds,

Find yourself that quiet place.
Wipe that tear from your tired face.
When your cares and woes just come too fast.
Hear your angel whisper, "Shh...Let it pass."

Angel Hymns

Listen on the whispering wind.
That's the lilt of an angel's hymn.
That gentle sigh, that tinkling chime.
Hush. Listen. It's the angel's time.

In the early evening hours
When the bees settle in the flowers,
All the angels gather near
To sing their hymns so we can hear.

The baby grins and shuts his eyes,
He's resting now. He does not cry.
That gentle sigh, that tinkling chime.
Hush. Listen. It's the angel's time.

Teen Angels

There are troubles out there along your way,
It's not like it was the other day
When Mom and Dad were in their schools
And measured by the golden rules.

Not so for you as life goes by
And you wonder whether to laugh or cry.
You think they'll surely throw you away,
For things have changed and are not so gay.

But you're not alone, not now, not ever.
Your angel waits and he's far more clever
Than that gangster lurking by your locker,
Or that bad dude who's the weapon's hawker.

School isn't like it used to be,
But your angel is and he comes for free.
So stop in the middle of it all,
Stop, and listen to your angel's call.

You're not alone. You never were.
Your angel's here, and he has the cure.
Look closer, you're not beneath the axe,
You won't be slipping through the cracks.

When everyone out there lets you down,
Don't hang your head and sit and frown.
Just remember that friend who knows your fears,
His wings are waiting to dry your tears.

Mother's Work

The day goes on without an end.
She folds the clothes, she stoops and bends.
She wonders as the hours go by
If she can stop before she cries.

It often gets her down a bit,
She could throw in the towel and just plain quit.
The kids come home and gripe and fight,
And hubby reads into the night.

She sits and sews. She cooks and cleans.
Does anyone notice how tired she seems?
She changes her clothes, climbs into bed.
Hubby plants a kiss on her tired head.

Her angel sees it all. He knows.
He sees her love, knows how it grows.
As she closes her eyes, sighs, and moans,
He leans and whispers, "You're not alone."

Father's Work

So deep the seas of discontent when all around are fine,
But there's a small and darkened space that I can call my mind,
Where no one goes and no one sees the fears that are inside.
I cover them with roses red, and blue and yellow skies.

For men it seems must bear the weight of all the outside world,
And make it seem that all is well, and goes on as it should.
But never once does anyone look deeper than the man,
And even bother to request if fear and darkness stand…

Between him and the life he lives from day unto the night,
While he toils on with daily work for family and might.
I reach without to all my friends and they in turn are kind.
They are the same as you and me, so all the troubles hide…

Down deep where no one knows the strength of all the darkened spaces,
Where bills and debts and worries wait and only time erases
The wear and tear upon my heart as I live day to day,
Acting like the world is grand, and everything is play.

But once or twice a thought does sink into the deeper realms.
And once or twice a message comes for higher, perfect ground.
And then I know the meaning of the songs of love I hear,
My wife, my children are my wealth, and nothing should I fear.

St. Francis and the Animals

He lies beneath the starry sky and waits for movement there,
And others of his brotherhood are full of rapture rare,
For there above a wondrous sight has come to bless their wait,
While angels dance and angels sing, and Heavenly Father plaits
A miracle of love and grace upon each brother's heart,
They have received His blessings full into their deepest part.
They lay all night beneath the stars and watch as if possessed.
Should any person happen by, they would sure be stressed
To see the seven brothers in a joyful rapture state,
And wonder what they're doing in this cold and darkened place?
How could they know that God himself had touched their hearts divine,
And in each one He placed a promise of his earthly climb.
And in each was a blessing of the joys of faith in Him,
And in each one a change had happened to his core within.
Then daylight came and with it dew, upon their tonsured heads.
They waken to the new day now and all the joys ahead.
They walk as if they are on clouds and nothing phases them.
And people pass and wonder why they sing and say, "Amen!"
Then in the day he finds a place, a bench to sit upon,
And as he sits the animals come so that they fair surround
This heavenly man, his kind heart bare to all of them right here,
A tiny bird it perches on his hand, then pecks his ear.
A little lamb lies down beside his blessed feet on sand,
And with a touch sweet love pours down to rest upon the lamb.
A deer advances timidly to see why they don't fear
This human as he sits and plays with all his kin so dear.

What is the difference in this man that they would come to him?
He sings, he plays, and offers them, innocence like a hymn.
And then the deer comes closer, so he sees the blessed smile,
And in its heart a light begins to glow and so beguile
That he must also come and be as close as he can be,
And feel the joy, the miracle that this monk brings hence to thee.
St. Francis sings and plays with them, and blesses every one.
He is the saint of animals true, but also, everyone.

She's an Angel

She gathers the pebbles and tosses the stones
Into the surf and out onto the foam.
The shells she holds fast in her beautiful hand.
And the waves bathe over her feet in the sand.

Along the shore in the noonday sunlight
She takes in the swimmers and the gulls in flight.
She drinks in the smells and the sounds and the breeze,
And remembers a times when she wasn't so free.

Her wings she spreads wide to the warm summer wind,
She flexes her arms and breathes it all in.
She's been here herself and remembers the time
When her whole life through was an uphill climb.

A hushed little breath escapes her sweet lips,
And her eyes mist over as she thinks of all this.
As if touched on her head by a magical wand
No one can see her. She's a step beyond.

Then a little boy smiles and looks up from his play,
He knew she was there, she'd been there all the day.
She was there when he slept, and again when he woke.
He could feel her heart beating though she never spoke.

He leaned to his mother and reached up to her ear
And whispered a secret for just her to hear,
And mother smiled back, glanced over her shoulder,
He nodded and giggled and pointed on over.

And the angel waved back and she blew him a kiss,
And his mother smiled too, she remembered all this,
When she was so tiny and so full of joy,
And she played with her angel like her little boy.

Then time passed on by like the thread through a needle,
And now she's a mother, where did all the years go?
Then he tottled on over to his angel friend
And they splashed in the water, playing...pretend.

Of Pillows

Pillows are neat and they're soft and they're white,
Like puffy, full clouds and the doves in flight.
They're made from the feathers of birds flying over
The land and the seas, and the castles on clover.

The clouds drift free o're the green of the land,
And the sky breathes a breath of love from its hand,
And the people look up, and they gaze on in wonder.
"Where did all the rain go, where is all the thunder?"

Then beyond the walls of the great castle keep,
The brave little prince reaches out in his sleep,
And he pulls it much closer 'neath his little head,
And the covers he kicks right off of his bed.

But the pillow, now that will not reach the cold floor,
It's held fast in his dreams where he's fighting the war.
He wields high his proud sword to the enemy king,
And the doves, they circle his head like a ring.

He's a righteous, proud leader, a king without fear,
Then a draft wafts over his legs small and bare.
And he pulls in his pillow 'neath his wee little head.
The one that makes kings in a small prince's bed.

Bella Bella, Alexia

I sit so quietly by the stream
Where others might just laze and dream.
But my thoughts are not within this place,
I've come for yet another space.

And then I see her, angel bright
With robes of glistening gold and white,
And hair that flows down to her sides,
And in her arms a baby hides.

She comes a little closer now,
As I stand up to greet her call.
And joy wells up within my heart,
For here I know is the missing part.

Helena is her name, she says,
And in her arms, a dear old friend,
Who long has waited for this day,
To come to earth, to have her say.

She waits within her baby dreams
All cuddled in her angel's wings.
She's safe and sound, and none would know
That soon a journey, long and slow
Will be her mission for us all…
When summer's here and robins call.

Then Helena bids me nearer still.
My heart wells up with tears to fill
An ocean or a world beyond.
There is no limit to my love.

"Is this our baby?" I ask now.
"The one we've waited for so long?
Is she the one to fill the wrong
That others left, without a song?"

And Helena reaches out to me,
An angel hand all golden, free,
And brushes it against my cheek
With love, and smiles, so I can't speak.

And then I know, and then I see,
As baby's eyes look out at me
From there within her angel's wings,
And my heart soars, as angels sing.

And then she came, July the sixth
Just as her angel, Helena, picked.
She chose this day all on her own,
So her dear friend would be at home.

Mama and Babba, now hold her
Closer, and closer yet, for sure.
And wrap around her all their love,
Just like Helena did above.

Alexia, our angel from above,
You brought the finest, deepest love
From highest, brightest, purest heaven,
Down here to earth for us to live in.

Little Bella, Bella dream
Who came from heaven by the stream,
There is no other, none so fair.
For you're the answer to our prayers.

Wake Up

Wake up today and look inside
Where all your hopes and fears do hide,
And find the treasure chest you've put
Deep down inside, a sealed-shut book.

Guardians angels read the pages,
Know the clues, they are the sages.
They know you do seek for sure
For all that's good and safe and pure.

But they can't do their work for you
And help you see the trials through,
If you don't lose your tight death grip
Upon the threads of this life's trip.

So dream yourself upon a pillow
Of satiny white and downy billow,
And rest there often in your mind,
And let the angels play their chimes.

Forgive yourself for all you've done,
And all the mis-creations gone.
Let go and let your angel's wings
Fly you up to better things.

Let go and let the blessings flow
From up above to down below.
And then you'll know why you are here,
And then your angels can come near.

Don't take the Maker's heavenly plans
Into your earthly, childlike hands.
He knows what's best here in this fog
So just let go. And then…Let God.

On an Angel's Wing

It's winter now and all is still.
The wind is blowing o'er the hill, and the trees they bend
In promised will, to the little one whose gaze it fills.
He knows it is his time to come.
He knows, and wills it as he runs
Along the clouds, across your dreams,
To brush your mind with angel wings.
He lifts his hand and blows a kiss.
To those he leaves, he sends a wish.
"I will return to you again,
But now my journey must begin."
They know, they smile and watch him pass
Through waters where the spirit lasts,
Into the one who's waiting there
To dry his tears and hush his cares.
Little do they realize
That he has magic in his eyes,
This little one with angel wings
Who sleeps so soundly as he grins.
A mighty force it builds inside,
Igniting light within his eyes
So he can see where others can't,
And calms the storms while others pant.
Many are there of his ilk,
They pass by us like golden silk,
And no one sees or hears or tells
The lofty message their bell knells.
"Come!" it says so loud and clear.
"Come and cast aside your fear!
We're here, and here we plan to stay

To usher in another day
Where love and laughter take your hand.
There is a true and promised land.
We've come to lead you to your place
With love and honor, peace and grace."
He sleeps, this little one of charms, within your warm
And loving arms; this Ancient One who's so profound
Rests now upon this hallowed ground.
This Ancient One so full of grace
Returns with honour to this place.

Sleep, Little One

Oh, I can hear the tinkling bells,
The tiny sounds, like little shells.
The swishing noise of silk on lace,
And the sweet little grin upon your face.

Your angel bends to blow a kiss,
Like a gentle breeze that you'll surely miss.
And crystals sing as the wind blows by,
In my mind I can hear a lullaby.

For love is wrapped around my heart,
And all the world is filled with stars.
Hush, little baby, sleep now, sleep.
Your loving angel keeps you safe.

Your Angel's Gifts

A whisper away behind a white cloud
She sits and writes her hopes all down
So she can lift the veil of tears,
And give to you some happy years.

She guards and guides, and prays and sighs,
And wishes you would let her try
To mend the fences, build the dreams,
And leave the sorrows with the schemes.

But there's a rhythm to her ways,
And there's a pattern that she paves.
Just look inside and you will know,
She'll reach through and help you grow.

But first you must look inside where
You weave your fears and dark despair,
And loss and greed and envy too.
You must search out these things anew.

And once you have them in your hand
Consider that the Maker's plan
Was set in motion long ago,
So you could learn, and you could grow,

And sometimes that will come with joy,
And sometimes with another toy
That may at first seem dark and deep,
But closer looks will prove they keep

And guard your secrets safe and sound,
So look within and they'll be found.
Forgive yourself for all you've done,
And then your angel gifts will come.

Forgive yourself for mis-creations
Because you have forced and bent the pieces
Of the puzzle from His plan.
Yourself, you did this, not His Hand.

Angels guard and guide and love,
And bring His love from up above.
So let them do their job for you.
Let go and let the good things through.

One Little Finger

With one little finger I count the stars.
With one little finger push aside the bars
That cover the midnight skies of blue.
One little finger to whisper to you.

With one little finger I could send a man flying.
With one little finger I can do all the tying.
And low and behold as I close my eyes,
With one little finger I say you are mine.

Count all the pebbles upon the shore twice,
Then count all the stars in the heavens yet thrice.
So many wonders will always be there,
But with one little finger, I have them all here.

For one little finger can point here and there.
And one little finger can say how I care.
One little finger says, "Wait, please, my pet."
For one little finger knows, it's not the time yet.

Lift up your eyes and count all the stars
Twinkling down on you from behind time's bars.
But one little finger is all that it takes,
To erase all the curtains that illusions do make.

This little finger says, "Not today, dear."
And this little finger says, "Hold that thought near."
For soon your heart knows that the order is given,
And one Mighty Finger will reach down from heaven

Commanding that all of our cares give way to
The blessings and gifts that His love sends anew
With His son on the morning of Easter again,
Then this little finger will bow with, Amen…

The Christmas King

The snows fall softly on the ground.
The shepherds come to gather round.
The air is cold and high above
A star shines brightly, full of love.

They are perplexed. They cannot know
That somewhere close, a miracle grows.
And somewhere near, the Lord of all,
Has come to answer love's great call.

Somewhere too a mother holds
The treasure that mankind must mold
Into the light of love and grace,
Within a tiny baby's face.

And then a mighty wind does blow
And whips the snow around them so
That they can scarcely see the star
That shines above them from afar.

And then the trumpet's sound are heard
And bells, and singing fill the earth.
The shepherds cry with mighty fear,
"Who is this messenger we have here?"

But lightly now the music chimes,
While angels sing their lullabies,
And lead the shepherds to a cave
Where baby Jesus has been lain.

And so they gather there to see
The King of all, who came to free
The souls of all mankind this day.
A tiny baby wrapped in hay.

Our Wedding Day

I dreamt I saw an angel bright, who stopped to talk to me.
Upon his lips a gentle smile, and in his hand, a key.
I asked him what the key was for, and softly he replied,
"It's so you'll know the one for you, the one that doesn't lie."

It's so you'll hear love's precious song and hold it to your heart;
Each living note will sing His praise, each chorus will impart
A message sent from up above that you've been waiting for.
This golden key you hold within will open up the door

It seemed a lifetime passed me by since first I held the key,
And then one day the heavens opened right in front of me,
And there you stood. You shook my world and sang to me a song,
A song I knew you'd sing to me throughout my whole life long.

And then one night I dreamt again about my angel friend.
He stood before me in His light, and he began to send
In beams of love, two heavenly doves, each in its beak a ring.
I asked him who the rings were for, what message do they bring?

And then you were beside me love, and in your hand my key.
The doves encircled round our heads and gave the rings to me.
And angels danced, and angels sang around us where we stood,
For all of heaven had opened up and bowed before our love.

Today we say our vows before our friends and families.
Today we open up the doors to our future bright and free.
Today all heaven celebrates a love that angels bring.
Today I give to you this ring. Today the angels sing.

Christmas Snow

A hush fell on the Christmas snow,
And all the angels bowed down low.
A whisper winged down from the star
That watched the couple traveling far.

And none could know and none could see
How long the grueling trip would be,
But deep inside the mother's womb
A glorious life was soon to bloom.

"No room!" they said at each full inn.
"No room for you to rest within."
And so they traveled on some more
To the welcoming farmer's open door.

"You may rest here if you like.
It's is the last place here this night,
But it is warm and it is clean
And you'll be comfortable it seems."

How could this humble farmer know
He'd rescued Jesus from the snow?
But he was kind, and he was blessed
To have the Saviour as his guest.

And then the light began to grow,
And from the heavens bright beams flowed,
And choruses came there from on high
When they first heard the Saviour sigh.

All of heaven opened its arms,
And all the stars were filled with charms.
Then Mary held Him close to her
And Joseph's heart was full and pure.

The small dark eyes with love did grow.
His parents' faces were aglow.
He smiled at them with heavenly love
As pure and sweet as a little dove.

So look ye not to times gone by
And ponder not how does it fly.
The wonder of His birth draws near,
So shed not even one small tear.

It is a miracle, so we hear
A wonder to recall each year,
To think of that sweet, glorious babe,
And give Him love and sing His praise.

To kiss that sweet, soft little cheek,
And hug that bundle long and deep,
And drink in all the wonderous love
That He brought with Him from above.

For love it lives in each small child
Just like the Saviour fair and mild.
It's good that all of us recall
The reason for this Christmas call…

The call to love and peace on earth.
The call to give each other worth.
The call to wish each mortal well.
The call to listen to the bells…

That ring, and chime from heaven's gate
While angels sing and mortals wait.
And baby Jesus comes again,
Each Christmas, like a long-lost friend.

Levi

Once a time ago it seems,
He stood within the altar's gleam,
And angels bowed their heads down low,
To see him guard his people so.

Candles flickered all around,
Their scent like blossoms on the ground,
For all were gathered round and near,
To hear the Father's message here.

They bow their heads in fervent prayer
While Levi drives away their cares.
And in their hearts he calms their fears
That have been building up for years.

He is the one, the priest most high,
And favored in the Father's eye.
They know this well for every day,
Levi leads them on their way.

They crossed the barren, sun-scorched land,
A staff of truth held in his hand.
His strength and love still guides them now.
They never doubted where or how.

He waits now 'neath the starry sky
And tears begin to fill his eyes,
And Father speaks beneath the wind,
And messages flow straight unto him.

"Be kind," says Levi to their hearts,
"And love all people. Do your part.
Bring heaven down upon this earth
And prove you are of royal birth.

For Sons of God are all you here,
So never worry, ponder, fear
That He forgets or doesn't care
For his children all alone down here."

A baby now, but not for long.
He comes to sing a sacred song,
For Levi is a priest inside
Where love, and peace, and angels guide.

Star Boy

Twinkle, twinkle, little star,
I don't wonder where you are,
Because I came not long ago
Right from your heart, your very soul.

I came with speed, and loft, and grace
Into this earthly, grounding space
To do my work in coming times
When bells will ring and music chime.

I came so that the world would know
That not so very long ago,
I lived. Yes, lived on distant stars
Where life is still beyond your words.

For where I come from there are moons;
There are seven, white and blue.
And in the evening at sunset
The phases calm a weary breast.

Times are changing here on earth,
A time that now is taking birth.
A time when earthlings travel far
Beyond our measures, to the stars.

And I'll be there to guide the way,
To greet my people on that day
When all at once, the skies will part
And lighten every waiting heart.

A brand new age will soon begin,
An age for which I wait and yearn.
And many a heart will ponder why
There are wondrous sights up in the skies.

On my world we always say there is
One truth to share. One truth to give.
And that truth sends a blinding call,
"Give once! Give well! And give your all!"

I come from where the water falls
In grand torrents down the walls
Of mountains grand to valley's grace,
And crystal cities built in space.

Wonders of such you've never seen,
But worry not my people, please.
For one day, not so far away
I'll take you there, and there you'll stay.

If such is what you really crave
Then watch, and wait with me, and pray,
For Versa my home is waiting too,
To wrap her loving arms 'round you.

And from this point way out in space
You leap and grow, and lead the race
To conquer spaces yet unseen,
And worlds beyond your wildest dreams.

So, twinkle, twinkle, little star,
Now we all know that you are.
And angels from far distant shores
Will live with us forevermore.

Easter Time

Little daisies blow in breezes
While the air lights up with love.
Little roses send their fragrance
By the angels from above.

And all around us is the music,
Angels singing heavenly songs,
Because the Saviour has arisen,
Bringing forth a brand new dawn.

Hearts and Flowers

A heart to love us all day long.
A smile to sing us special songs.
And clear bright eyes to drink us in,
And fill us to the very brim.

Baby snuggles on your shoulder.
Angels watch us as we hold her.
And love surrounds us all the time,
Our little angel Valentine.

A Pot of Gold

They say you'll find a pot of gold
Beneath the rainbow, so we're told.
But I see one before my eyes,
An angel-leprechaun, disguised.

Gold dust fills the air around her.
A halo crowns her head of curls.
And lucky charms tell all the rest,
So, are we lucky? Or are we blessed?

Dancing Raindrops

April showers bring May flowers,
But we've a time to wait until
The little buds show forth their colors,
And little birds perch on the hills.

Drip, drip, drop, they fall around us,
But angels only laugh and sing
While watching little happy raindrops
Covering each and every thing.

For rain is but a little whisper
Of promises yet to come our way,
And so she sits, and sings, then slumbers,
Waiting for the flowers of May.

Angel Kisses

What is that sparkle on your cheek?
I saw it there and had to speak.
And there, above your eye I see
Another sits, and winks with glee.

Upon your shoulder there's a light,
If I look closer then I might
Just see it clearer, then I'll know
What is this sparkling lighting show.

You're glowing like a radiant sun!
And all around you there is spun
A silver thread that glints and hugs,
To wrap you in a cozy rug.

And now the stars fill up you face!
What is the meaning of this case?
But wait again, I look and see
An angel smiling back at me.

She leans down low to kiss your brow
And there! Another star does glow.
Such love I see before my face,
Such endless, boundless joy, and grace.

You're loved much more than you can know.
The sparkles on your face they show
That angels love you endlessly,
With kisses from an timeless sea.

An Angel Caper

The wind was gusting miles high, and everywhere was grey,
With dust and papers, leaves and branches, till we breathed the clay.
I opened up my car door fast against the howling gale,
And in that second from my hand it grabbed my precious mail.

A picture I had set aside for more time than I recall
Had finally come to light again so I answered to its call;
A precious photo it surely was of Grandma and her sister.
The only one that time had left without the cracks and blisters.

But the wind it blew, and the traffic too, as it flew across the road,
And there was no way I could get to there from where I was.
So I said a prayer as I always do, a prayer unto my angel.
"Please put you foot upon the sheet, and hold it 'til I get there!"

And off I went far down the street to cross with all the traffic.
How could this be? What was the use? The wind already had it.
"But faith!" the angel voice inside had shouted in my head.
"I'll get it for you, never fear, just cross the road ahead."

And so I crossed right at the light, followed all the signs as given,
Right up the street to where the photo last had made its prison.
I bent, and peered through every garden, 'neathe every car that parked there,
But not a whiff of my sweet Grandma, or of her little sister.

And then the kindest lady pulled into her drive nearby,
And saw that I was searching hard, and so she came to try
To see if there was anything that her kind heart could do,
To help this crazed, and wind-blown lady follow all the clues.

I explained what it was that brought me to her door.
She smiled and without even glancing back said,
"It's happened here before. Never ceases to amaze how things will end up here,
So let's just take a closer look around the side, my dear."

As we headed down along her walk I stopped in sheer amazement.
There was my photo caught between her fence and the dry pavement!
With all my heart I thanked her so she must think me crazed.
But in my mind I knew the truth. My angel saved the day.

Remembering

I hear the flutter of the pages, light and without care.
And as I look I chance to see an angel standing there.
And in his hand I see a book that's opened at a part,
And with his finger he shows me a secret from his heart.

My eyes can scarcely understand the meaning of the words.
I read it once, and yet again until the meaning stirs
A memory of long ago in far-off distant lands,
And then I know, and then I see his glowing angel hand…

Pointing back through all the years of centuries gone by,
To where the baby Jesus slept, with closed and peaceful eyes.
And in that moment I recalled a bliss not since recalled,
And then I knew that all of us remember all His calls…

If only we can understand that life here is a gift,
And only then can we begin to gather all the bliss
That's stored for us within His heart, so full of grace and love,
And only then will we remember heaven up above.

So worry not that life is all for worry and for strife.
And worry not that no joy comes without a long, hard fight.
Relax and let the hardships go, instead look deep within,
And you will see, and you will know, the answers are with Him.

I wish you peace. I wish you love in all the darkened spaces,
So it will grow and fill the void that fear often erases.
I wish you honesty and love, and all good things for sure,
But mostly I wish hope for you; a life of shining pearls.

Printed in the United States
39165LVS00013B/127-132

9 781413 784220